Piglets

Julie Murray

Abdo Kids Junior
is an Imprint of Abdo Kids
abdobooks.com

Abdo
BABY ANIMALS
Kids

abdobooks.com

Published by Abdo Kids, a division of ABDO, P.O. Box 398166, Minneapolis, Minnesota 55439.

Printed in the United States of America, North Mankato, Minnesota.

102018

012019

Photo Credits: Alamy, iStock, Shutterstock

Production Contributors: Teddy Borth, Jennie Forsberg, Grace Hansen

Design Contributors: Christina Doffing, Candice Keimig, Dorothy Toth

Library of Congress Control Number: 2018946166

Publisher's Cataloging-in-Publication Data

Names: Murray, Julie, author.

Title: Piglets / by Julie Murray.

Description: Minneapolis, Minnesota : Abdo Kids, 2019 | Series: Baby animals set 2 | Includes glossary, index and online resources (page 24).

Identifiers: ISBN 9781532181672 (lib. bdg.) | ISBN 9781532182655 (ebook) | ISBN 9781532183140 (Read-to-me ebook)

Subjects: LCSH: Piglets--Juvenile literature. | Baby animals--Juvenile literature. | Domestic animals--Infancy--Juvenile literature. | Pigs--Juvenile literature.

Classification: DDC 636.407--dc23

Table of Contents

Piglets

Most **female** pigs have 6 to 12 piglets at a time.

They weigh 3 pounds (1.4 kg) at birth.

They are pink in color.

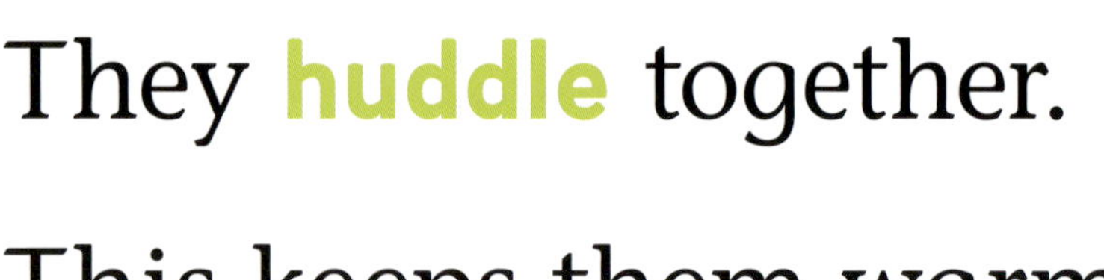

They **huddle** together.

This keeps them warm.

They drink their mother's milk.

Soon they will eat **grains** too.

Piglets grow quickly!

At 2 months, they weigh

40 pounds (18 kg).

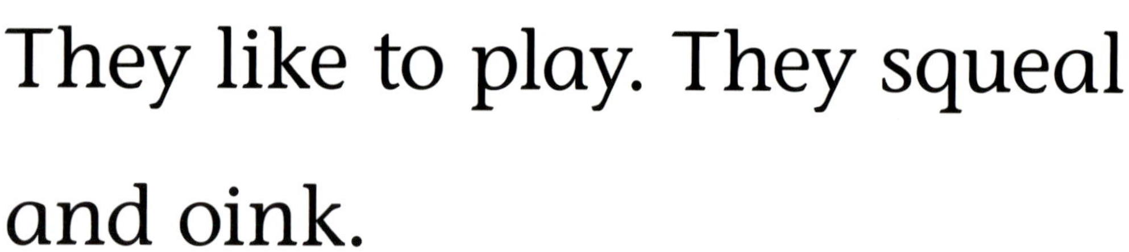

They like to play. They squeal and oink.

Piglets like to roll in the mud.

This keeps them cool.

Watch a Piglet Grow!

newborn

1 month

2 months

6 months

Glossary

grain
the small, hard seeds of cereal plants such as wheat or rice.

female
a girl animal that can have young.

huddle
to push in against one another when sharing something such as heat.

Index

Visit **abdokids.com** and use this code to access crafts, games, videos, and more!

Abdo Kids Code:
BPK1672